Einstein

Ambujam Anantaraman

Einstein
New Horizon Media ©

First Edition: August 2008
64 Pages
Printed in India.

ISBN 978–81–8368–915–1
Pro–ya–en–19

Prodigy Books
177/103, First Floor,
Ambal's Building, Lloyds Road,
Royapettah, Chennai 600 014.
Ph: +91-44-4200-9603

Email : support@nhm.in
Website : www.nhm.in

Author's Email: ambujama@gmail.com

Contents

Introduction

'My dear children, I rejoice to see you before me today, happy youth of a sunny and fortunate land. Bear in mind that the wonderful things you learn in your schools are the work of many generations, produced by enthusiastic effort and infinite labour in every country of the world. All this is put into your hands as your inheritance in order that you may receive it, honour it, add to it and one day faithfully hand it over to your children. Thus do we mortals achieve immortality in the permanent things, which we create in common? If you always keep that in mind, you will find a meaning in life, and work and acquire the right attitude towards other nations and ages' – Albert Einstein, 1934

Albert Einstein, one of the greatest scientists of all time, was once asked to appear with Charlie Chaplin, the master entertainer, during the opening of the film *City Lights* in Hollywood. Thousands of people mobbed them. Charlie Chaplin told Einstein rather cheekily, 'The people applaud me because everybody understands me, and they applaud you because no one understands you.'

Such was the complicated nature of the science that this Nobel laureate taught this world. He was a theoretical physicist.

Physics is about the laws of nature. Some laws are demonstrated experiments in the laboratory. There are brilliant people, who understand these laws and write them down in the form of mathematic formulae. Einstein was foremost among such people.

With his Theories of Relativity, his explanation of the photoelectric effect and his theory of the origin of the universe, Einstein explained many vital physical phenomena to fellow human beings.

Einstein was a great scientist but also a very special man who spent his life trying to teach people the value of peace. He was totally against war.

He was a humanist—interested in ideas relating to religion, truth, and non-violence. In all these thoughts, he was inspired by Gautama Buddha, Mahatma Gandhi and Rabindranath Tagore.

Einstein did not have a perfect life. Like many scientists, he was quite stubborn in his personal and professional views and relationships. He married twice and one of his sons was mentally ill. His last days were not very peaceful. More and more theories were being proposed in science and he could not fully agree with them. He was sad because one of his theories led to the invention of the atom bomb.

Einstein's dream was to have a 'theory of everything'. And scientists are definitely proceeding towards that goal!

Einstein's Life and Times

The early years of Einstein never gave a clue as to what was to come in the future. He was not exactly a child prodigy. He was rather the opposite. His life story is an inspiration to one and all because it shows how poor performance at school need not deter a genius from blooming.

Albert Einstein was born at a place called Ulm in Wurttemberg in Germany on 14 March, 1879. He was the first child of Hermann and Pauline Einstein. His father was a businessman and his mother a pianist.

Apparently, his mother was frightened by the uncommon shape of the child's head, and his grandmother thought the baby was simply too heavy. They even feared the child was not normal, as he took too long to speak.

In 1881, his mother gave birth to a daughter, Maria. Maja, as Einstein called her, was the person he was closest to in his life. His parents were Jews. They were liberal by nature and there was no strict observance of religious ritual in his house. For instance, Einstein never underwent the *Bar Mitzvah*. Jews consider this an essential ritual somewhat like baptism in Christianity.

In his early years Einstein was a loner. He had a marked tendency to throw tantrums, which included hurling things at his sister. At other times he was totally gentle. In other words, his complex personality was evident even then.

Einstein's mother taught him to play the violin. His father read stories to the two children. The boy did not like outdoor games and preferred to stay at home. He used to build houses of cards with infinite patience. He disliked physical games and was poor in gymnastics and other sports. Once, his parents took him to witness a military parade. Much to their shock, the young Albert took ill at seeing the men march in a stiff column. Later in life he said that the sight of seeing men forced to do something their brains did not want to do was disturbing in the extreme. Such was his aversion to the military and things associated with war. He was extremely scared that he would be drafted for compulsory military service in Switzerland. Luckily for him, he was found medically unfit because he suffered from varicose veins.

The first indication of Albert's great future as a man of science came when he was five, when his father gave him a pocket compass. Albert thought he was seeing a miracle. The compass moved only in the northern direction whichever way it was held and this fascinated him. Not many five-year-olds would have been so observant.

When Albert was six, the family moved to Munich, where he began his schooling. Though many people have said that he was a poor student, he was a topper in studies, especially in mathematics and Latin.

In 1890, after being exposed to religious education for the first time in his life, he went through an intense religious phase, when he composed songs on God. He used to sing them to himself while walking to school!

Einstein was fond of music and geometry. His uncle influenced him greatly, and encouraged young Albert's interest in mathematics by giving him books to read. He called the book of Euclidean Geometry his Holy Book. Between the ages of 12 and 16, he studied integral and differential calculus (very difficult subjects!) by himself.

By 1894, things changed. The business Albert's father ran along with his brothers began to suffer and the family decided to move to Italy where the brothers felt the business might fare better. While the family moved to Milan, Albert stayed back at Munich to finish school.

He could not bear to be away from his family and he left school without finishing his course, to join them at Pavia.

Fortunately, Einstein decided the very next year to pursue further education and sat for the entrance exam to the ETH or the Federal Institute of Technology, Zurich. Unfortunately, he did not make the grade. After this, he studied at a school in Aarau for a year and obtained a diploma in 1900. This qualified him to enrol in the ETH for a course that would entitle him to teach maths and physics in high schools. A little earlier, in 1896, he had given up his German citizenship and became a Swiss citizen.

Despite his brilliance and intelligence, Einstein had to face the problem of unemployment for two years after passing out of the ETH. His teacher disliked him because he felt he was too independent-minded. So, he did not help him to find a job. Einstein had to try and make a living by giving tuitions in mathematics and physics to young children studying in small schools. He did not find this challenging, and perhaps because of that, was somewhat indifferent. Time and again Einstein was sacked even from these small jobs.

Poor Einstein! At this point he was feeling miserable that he was not able to help his parents and had in fact become a burden to the family.

After a couple of temporary teaching assignments, he finally got help from his classmate and life-long friend Marcel Grossmann. He became a technical assistant at the patent office, in Berne at a nominal salary. In the patent office Einstein's job was to assess whether an invention in the area of electrical machinery was worthy of a patent.

A patent is a right granted by a government to an inventor for an invention. This right forbids any one else from using or making use of the invention without the inventor's permission. Einstein was so good at his work that he used to complete the work assigned to him by forenoon. In the afternoons, he spent his time writing scholarly papers on physics!

He worked in the patent office till 1909, when he was able to embark on a full time career as a scientist and physics professor. Unbelievably, it was during this period that he did his best scientific work!

With a job and salary, Albert married his classmate Mileva Maric in 1903. Mileva was the only female student in his class, and Einstein referred to her as his equal and partner in all respects.

In 1905, which has been called the Miracle Year, Einstein published four ground-breaking papers in physics in a journal called Annalen Der Physik. These papers were revolutionary and presented a new explanation of physical phenomena that guided the universe. The papers were on 1 Photoelectric effect. 2 Brownian motion. 3 Electrodynamics and 4 Equivalence of matter and energy. It was in the fourth paper that Einstein explained his famous formula $E = mc^2$.

Probably because Einstein was not with a university, these remarkable papers came to the attention of other physicists only after considerable passage of time. Gradually, Einstein's contemporaries began to recognise the originality of his work.

Meanwhile, he got his PhD from Berne University, studying part-time. This was his first and only earned PhD. Almost all the great universities of the world such as Oxford, Cambridge, and Harvard later conferred honorary doctorates on him.

As the scientific world came to grips with the significance of his work, universities vied with one another to take him into their fold. After brief stints in the Universities of Prague and ETH, Zurich, Einstein settled down as a Professor in Berlin. He was not very fond of teaching as it required him to put things down in an orderly way making notes of lessons and monitoring the progress of his students. Einstein found that such routine work interrupted his flow of thought. His thought flow was like a torrent or waterfall. How could you stop a waterfall from flowing continuously?

Later, the Berlin University relieved him of his teaching responsibilities so that he could concentrate on research.

Unfortunately, during this time, Einstein was having troubles in his married life. After much deliberation, Albert and Mileva decided to separate and in 1914. Mileva moved to Zurich with their two sons, while Einstein continued at Berlin as Professor and Director of the Kaiser Wilhelm Institute for Physics. Separation from the family caused much distress to Einstein, and he cried on the way back from the railway station to his apartment, after dropping them off on a train to Zurich.

Einstein was suffering from a liver ailment and was advised to be on a very strict diet. He needed someone to look after him. His first cousin Elsa Lowenthal, who had two daughters by an earlier marriage, moved in to look after him. They got along very well and Einstein married Elsa in 1919 after divorcing Mileva. He promised her that if he were ever to win the Nobel Prize—he had already been nominated several times—he would give her the prize money.

By 1920, he recovered from his ailment and visited the United States in 1921 to raise funds to set up a Hebrew University in Jerusalem. The President of the United States, Warren Harding, held a reception for him at the

White House. He received the Nobel Prize for Physics in 1921 for his services to theoretical physics, especially for his discovery of the photoelectric effect.

He continued his work on complicated aspects of physics connected with Quantum Theory and Unified Field Theory. In 1928, he was awarded the Max Planck medal for his contributions to Quantum Physics. While receiving the award he humbly said he had contributed nothing but occasional insights to quantum physics in the course of 'fruitless struggles with the main problem.'

Einstein was appointed a professor in the Institute of Advanced Studies in Princeton in America in 1932. His original idea was to divide his time evenly between Berlin and Princeton. He left Berlin that year to take up the position in Princeton, intending to return home the next year. Meanwhile, the cloud of Nazism was gathering in Germany and in 1933, the Nazis came to power. They raided Einstein's summer home in Kaput to look for arms hidden by the Communist Party. Soon after, Einstein resigned from the Prussian Academy of Sciences and never returned to Berlin.

The genocide of the Jews upset him immensely. He was outspoken in his criticism. He did not take up arms and remained a pacifist — committed to peace.

After the Second World War, when the state of Israel was born, leaders including the Prime Minister of Israel offered the presidency of the new country to Einstein. Suffering from very poor health, he declined the offer.

The last two decades of Einstein's life were mainly spent in academic work and in campaigning for a world without war.

One person who stood by him through thick and thin was his younger sister Maria. She held a doctorate in Romance Languages and moved to Princeton, where she lived near Einstein's home. Elsa and his two step-daughters were with him till he passed away in 1955 of a heart ailment.

Albert Einstein was cremated in Princeton and his ashes were strewn in an undisclosed location. Of his two sons, the eldest, Harns obtained a PhD in Technical Sciences from ETH, Zurich and became a Professor at the University of Berkeley, California. His other son Edward, who suffered from schizophrenia, was admitted in a mental asylum in Switzerland. This caused much grief to Einstein.

Einstein and the Nobel Prize

Albert Einstein won the Nobel Prize, the most important award in science, in 1921. It was awarded to him 'for his services to theoretical physics and especially for his explanation of the photoelelectric effect.'

Alfred Nobel, the father of the Nobel Prize, one day found to his utter surprise a news item about his death, when he was very much alive! This paper had earlier criticised him for his discovery of dynamite, an explosive that can kill or harm people.

After reading the death notice, Nobel decided to leave his entire fortune to be given away as prizes to achievers in five different subjects—physical sciences, chemistry, medical science or physiology, literary work and peace. Many more subjects were added later.

The value of the money left in his will was about four million US dollars, which has today grown to several billion US dollars.

Apart from the money, a gold medallion and a diploma are also given. The prizes were instituted in 1895 and first awarded in 1901.

The first physics prize went to Wilhelm Conrad Roentgen, who discovered X-ray. It is given away every year on the death anniversary of Alfred Nobel, December 10 in Stockholm by the Royal Swedish Academy of Sciences.

Einstein happened to be one of the few Nobel prize winners who did not attend the award ceremony! In September 1922, a friend wrote to him that he had a strong chance for the 1921 Physical Sciences Prize and wondered if he would postpone his plan to travel to Japan in the winter. Perhaps because many previous nominations had been unfruitful, Einstein went ahead on the long sea trip to the Far East with Elsa. The telegram intimating him about the prize landed at his Berlin home on November 10, 1922. It is not known when Einstein heard the news.

It was decided that a representative would receive the award on his behalf. Confusion followed! The German Ambassador to Sweden was invited by the academy authorities to collect the prize. Meanwhile, the Swiss

Ambassador claimed he was the right person as Einstein was a Swiss citizen! Communications went back and forth till it was decided that the German would receive the honour. The Ambassador, Rudolph Nadolny, made his speech most tactful. He referred to, 'the joy of my people that once again one of them has been able to achieve something for all mankind.... I hope that Switzerland also, which during many years provided the scholar a home and opportunities to work, will participate in this joy.'

The confusion did not end there. Who was to hand over the medal to Einstein after he returned in 1923? The Germans or the Swiss? Both countries again staked a claim. A compromise was reached. The Swedes intervened and decided to present the medal themselves. The Swedish Ambassador to Germany gave it to the elusive Einstein in Berlin. Einstein did go to Sweden in July 1923. Instead of the traditional acceptance speech, he delivered a lecture on the Theory of Relativity! Significant, because the Nobel intimation specifically said that he was not being given the award for the Theory of Relativity as it had not been confirmed yet. Of course, it was proved later and Einstein is today famous for it.

During the selection process, which went before all this, the five-member Nobel committee received nominations in Einstein's name right from 1910 onwards. He was nominated no less than 11 times, and he was finally picked for the 1921 prize.

Among the prominent scientists who nominated Einstein was Chemistry Nobel Laureate Wilhelm Ostwald. He repeated the nomination in 1912 and 1913, when he was joined by W Wien (Physics – 1911). Strangely, all these nominations were for the Theory of Relativity. Moving a decade forward, Max Planck (Physics – 1918) and Carl Wilhelm Oseen nominated Einstein for relativity and the photoelectric effect respectively. The committee gave two notable scientists the job of studying Einstein's contributions in each of these fields. While the first criticised the theory of relativity, the second felt experimentalists should be honoured for work on the photoelectric effect. Finally, no physics prize was awarded in 1921.

Planck did not give up and neither did Oseen. The next year, Planck suggested that the 1921 prize be given to Einstein and the 1922 award to Bohr. Many other big names joined in. The same scientist again came down heavily on relativity, but fortunately Oseen gave a magnificent analysis of Einstein's papers on the photoelectric effect.

It worked! The Nobel Committee proposed Einstein and the full Academy voted in his favour.

Einstein gave the prize money to his first wife Mileva Maric as promised.

He also won the Copley Medal and the Max Planck Medal. The first is awarded by the Royal Society of London to distinguished scientists in physics and biology, in alternating years. It is much older than the Nobel Prize, having been established using a grant from a landowner called Sir Geoffrey Copley, as early as 1731. It is the highest award given by the Royal Society of London. Einstein got the award in 1925.

This was soon followed by the Max Planck medal. Max Planck, himself a Nobel Laureate, was one of the first to recognise Einstein's scientific genius. He and his friend were jointly awarded the medal by the German Physical Society in 1929.

Scientific Achievements
Theory of Relativity

It followed from the special theory of relativity that mass and energy are both but different manifestations of the same thing—a somewhat unfamiliar conception for the average mind. Furthermore, the equation $E = mc^2$, *in which energy is put equal to mass, multiplied by the square of the velocity of light, showed that very small amounts of mass may be converted into a very large amount of energy and vice versa.*

That is how Einstein defined the Special Theory of Relativity.

Though he won the Nobel Prize for another concept in physics, Einstein is best known for his Special and General Theories of Relativity, proposed by him in the early part of the 20th century in one of the most significant scientific advances of our time.

Einstein was not the first person to introduce the concept of relativity though. That credit goes to Galileo, whom we know as the inventor of the telescope! Galileo lived in the 16th Century, more than 300 years before Einstein.

His principle of relativity stated that all laws of physics are the same for all observers in uniform motion, relative to one another. In other words, if two people are walking at the same speed, and if a vehicle passes by next to them, the time it will take for both persons to see the back of the vehicle will be the same.

Einstein's Special Theory of Relativity was an advancement on this basic theory. He realised that the speed of light in a vacuum is constant and an absolute physical boundary for motion. Nothing can move faster than light and light always travels at the same speed in a vacuum. A vacuum is a region where there is no air. This does not have a major impact on a person's day to day life, as we travel at speeds much slower than light. However, for objects travelling near the speed of light, the Theory of Relativity states that these objects will move slower and shorten in length from the point of view of someone looking from Earth. As something moves closer to you, it will look shorter and shorter!

Of course, this is only an effect. The real length of the object does not vary, nor does its speed.

Einstein published these ideas in famous papers in the year 1905, and they caused great excitement in the scientific community. 1905 was the wonderful year in Einstein's life as he came up with so many path-breaking ideas!

Using the Special Theory of Relativity, Einstein also derived the famous equation, $E = mc^2$, which shows the equivalence of mass and energy.

Equivalence does not mean the same as equal. This expression means that every mass has some energy associated with it, and every form of energy has some mass. In essence, it means mass is just one form of energy. E stands for energy, m for mass (how much a body weighs in space, where there is no gravity) and c is the speed of light. Mass and energy can be converted into each other! In relativity, mass and energy are two forms of the same thing, and neither appears without the other. When a body has a mass, it has a certain amount of energy, even when it is not moving. Similarly, even a really small moving object, like a photon (a small particle of light) has a mass, even when it is moving.

This theory is very important because it brings together two of the most important universal laws—the conservation of mass and the conservation of energy. Conservation means that mass or energy can neither be created nor destroyed, but only converted from one form to another.

The mass–energy equivalence formula was used in the development of the atom bomb.

An atom is a small particle of matter. It has a nucleus or centre, surrounded by small particles called electrons. The nucleus itself is made up of more small particles called protons and neutrons. The nucleus is held together by a form of energy called binding energy. By measuring the mass of the nucleus and subtracting from that the total mass of protons and neutrons, the extra mass present in the nucleus as binding energy is obtained. This formula is used to calculate the energy released in any nuclear reaction. A nuclear reaction occurs when two nuclei interact. An atomic bomb is a type of nuclear reaction that releases large amounts of energy. It has terrible consequences and after this was realised, no country has ever used the atom bomb in warfare. Still, many countries have the capacity to make bombs and some have kept them ready for use in an emergency.

Let us now move to the General Theory of Relativity. It is a theory of gravitation developed by Einstein in 1915. Gravity, as we know, is the pull that the earth exerts on all objects. Other objects in the Universe too have gravity.

It is based on the same mass-energy equivalence concept. When Einstein applied it to gravitational fields, he came up with some exciting results. He found that 'space' and 'time' were inseparable entities. He said space and time were linked together to form a continuous two-dimensional surface that was present everywhere in the Universe. How does this Spacetime look—Straight? Round? Curved?

First, he said Spacetime could be 'straight' only when it did not have anything in it. This is not the case. The Universe has numerous objects which have mass. Where there is mass, there will be gravity. Now, when there is gravity, there will be a curve. This curve, which we can compare to a slide in a playground, has an effect on how an object like a star or a planet will move in space.

Gravity, according to Einstein, is the curvature of space! This is somewhat different from the theory proposed by Isaac Newton. It is not that Newton was wrong, but rather that Einstein was more correct!

There is a common example used to explain this theory. Imagine if we were to take a large rubber sheet made up of two kinds of rubber stitched together. Let one kind be space and the other time. Now if you throw a large ball on the sheet, there would be a depression where the ball landed. This is exactly what Einstein said—the two dimensional time-space surface (the rubber sheet) is disrupted by gravity (the large ball) to create dips.

This aspect of relativity is so important because it explained the phenomenon of light bending around the sun, predicted black holes in space as well as the background radiation left from the Big Bang.

The sun, as we know, is at the centre of the solar system, and planets like Earth, Mercury, Mars and so on circle it. The sun is a star which emits light and heat. It is very heavy and has very strong gravity. Light, as we said earlier, is made up of small particles called photons. When these small particles found everywhere in space come close to the sun, they are pulled by the sun's gravity. How do we see these particles? As rays of light. These rays bend around the sun.

Remember, Einstein was a theoretical physicist. He found out all this by sheer thinking and analysis. Experimental physicists were the ones who tested these theories.

After a delay caused by the first Word War, two expeditions undertook the task of testing Einstein's theory of deflected star light near the sun, by conducting experiments. One set sail for an island called Principe off the coast of West Africa, while another went to a place called Sobral in the northern part of Brazil. They observed the solar eclipse that occurred on May 19, 1919 and found that Einstein's theories were correct.

In November that year, the results were announced at a joint meeting of the Royal Society and the Royal Astronomical Society in London. The President of the former, J J Thomson, himself a Nobel Laureate, said, 'This result is not an isolated one, it is a whole continent of scientific ideas. This is the most important result obtained in connection with the theory of gravitation since Newton's day.'

The headline in the Times of London said, 'Revolution in Science—New Theory of the Universe—Newton's Ideas Overthrown—Momentous Pronouncement—Space 'Warped.'

Einstein became famous and was invited to give lectures all over the world. In 1921, he began a tour of the United States, England, Japan, and France. Crowds came to listen to him in thousands.

The oldest picture of Einstein

Albert Einstein as a boy

Einstein 1921

Citizen Einstein

1919 eclipse positive

Scientific Achievements
Theory of Relativity II

What were the other mysteries that Einstein's General Theory of Relativity helped unravel? We mentioned Black Holes and the Big Bang. We can add cosmology too.

We said, when Einstein came up with the General Theory of Relativity, he realised that 'space' and 'time' were inseparable entities, and that this Spacetime was curved. We saw an example of how this Spacetime resembles a rubber sheet.

We also talked about how, if a massive object like the sun is placed on the sheet, it will bend. The more heavy an object is, the deeper the depression it makes in Spacetime. Suddenly a point is reached when the walls of the depression are stretched so steeply that nothing can climb out of it. It is like a hole in the universe.

This is exactly what a black hole is. It has very strong gravity that prevents the escape of any object that enters it, even light!

Einstein predicted black holes long before they were observed by using sophisticated instruments like telescopes! Einstein himself could not believe that such an invisible entity as a black hole could exist in the real universe, beyond his theories. However, today we know that black holes are found in space, far outside the solar system. They have a gravity of their own, which is very strong. A black hole absorbs all matter coming near it. It is totally dark as it emits no light. That is why it is called a black hole.

Einstein's relativity equations have also helped us understand the origins of the Universe. His equations predicted that the universe is dynamic and expanding. And, they also suggested that many millions of years ago, our Universe was created from a single dot in space! Scientists believe that a Big Bang caused the creation of the Universe. It is called the Big Bang because it is thought that many millions of years ago, all matter was in one dense form that was very hot. Around 15,000 million years ago, there was an explosion in this dense form and several galaxies were created. Galaxies are collections of stars and planets. Our galaxy is called the Milky Way.

Springing from the General Theory of Relativity was a science called cosmology. Cosmology is a field that tries to understand the physical universe as a unified whole by combining the study of natural sciences like physics and astronomy. Einstein's equations said that the universe is dynamic—expanding. This contradicted the prevailing view that the universe was static, so he reluctantly introduced a 'cosmological term' to stabilise his model of the universe. This he called a cosmological constant.

In 1929 astronomer Edwin Hubble found that the universe was indeed expanding, confirming Einstein's theory that the universe was dynamic. In 1930, Einstein met Hubble and told him that the cosmological constant was his 'greatest blunder.' Soon thereafter, the cosmological constant was dropped from most theories about the Universe.

Science grows and changes. In keeping with that trend, recent satellite data has shown that the cosmological constant is not irrelevant. A new theory has been proposed that the Universe, when it was very young, went through a rapid phase of inflation. After that it became more or less flat. When we have a ball of clay, and we want to make it flat, we have to use some energy to smoothen it out. Similarly, to make the Universe flat, some amount of energy (and its other form mass!)

would have been required. When astronomers measure the amount of matter and energy in the universe today they only come up with about 30 per cent of what is needed to make the universe flat. The cosmological constant is thought to be the remaining 70 per cent. What Einstein believed to be his biggest mistake has become an exciting field of exploration today! Some scientists even feel that the 'blunder' may determine the ultimate fate of the Universe.

Scientific Achievements
The Photoelectric Effect

Many of us wonder what light is made of. You can see it but you cannot feel it! You certainly can't catch it! Light was a topic of great discussion in the early 20th century. Some scientists stated that light was composed of waves. They said that light energy moved down to earth from space in the form of waves, rather like water in the sea comes to the shore as waves. Light waves were thought to be a type of electromagnetic waves. Waves crashing on a beach and electromagnetic waves or light do have some thing in common. For example, the highest point in both types of waves is called a peak, and the lowest point is a trough. The distance between two peaks is called the wavelength. The big difference is what these waves are made of! While we know waves in the sea are made up of moving water, it is much harder to tell what an electromagnetic wave is made of.

The wave, or 'disturbance,' is in an invisible thing called the electric force field. The electric force field arises because of the interaction between small particles. It is this force that helps light travel through air.

There was much experimental support for the theory that light was made up of waves. One phenomenon was not explained by the wave theory. This was the photoelectric effect. Some scientists noticed that when light fell upon a metal surface, small particles called electrons were emitted or ejected from the surface. They called this the photoelectric effect. Many scientists tried to find an explanation for this, and one of them, Max Planck came up with a mathematical equation. In his equation, Planck assumed that the energy in light waves did not act continuously, as explained in the wave theory, but existed in small, equal packets, or 'quanta,' of energy. This theory seemed to contradict the widely-accepted wave theory of light. However, Planck did not think that this was actually possible in the real world! He believed that he had just come up with a mathematical trick to explain the photoelectric effect.

It was Einstein who conclusively explained that light actually consisted of individual 'quanta' or packets of energy. These quanta are called photons now. The waves, which had been seen in many experiments, were nothing but the sum of many quanta. With his light quantum hypothesis Einstein was able to explain the photoelectric effect.

Light quanta, acting like little particles, can easily eject electrons. They simply knock them out of the surface of a metal. Imagine that you have a table with many bottles arranged on it. If you throw a ball at one of the bottles, the force from the ball will knock the bottle from the table. Similarly, the photons in the light knock the electrons off the metal surface. In scientific terms, this means that the energy contained in the light is absorbed by electrons within the metal. This gives sufficient energy for electron emission from the surface of the metal.

There was another question surrounding the photoelectric effect that Einstein solved. According to the classical wave theory, when the light that falls on the metal is more intense, the emitted electrons have greater energy. However, in some experiments it was seen that the energy of the emitted electrons are independent of the intensity of light. Therefore, the experimental evidence in this case did not agree with the theory, a scientific paradox.

Einstein successfully resolved this paradox in 1905. He said the intensity of light and the energy of the emitted electron had no relationship with each other. Increased intensity resulted in more electrons being emitted but did not change their energy.

Both these predictions were confirmed experimentally! The photoelectric effect is perhaps the most direct and convincing evidence of the existence of photons. It is considered a revolutionary discovery that has today led to the widely accepted 'wave-particle' theory of light.

This means that light often behaves as a wave, but when it comes into contact with any matter, it functions as if it is made up of small particles called photons. This is known as the dual nature of light.

Other Scientific Achievements

Einstein made many more notable contributions to the field of physics. In 1905, Einstein published a paper on Brownian motion. Robert Brown, a British botanist, while studying pollen grains, had observed that they moved continuously when they were put in water. This came to be called Brownian motion.

We can describe it in another way. Look at a glass of water sitting on a dining table. It seems to be perfectly still, right? However, the water molecules are actually moving continuously!

Brownian motion is therefore the random movement of small particles in liquids. Einstein gave a theoretical explanation for what had been observed in an experiment. He said the random movement of very small objects was direct evidence of molecular action. Molecules are made up of atoms. Einstein's paper was important as it supported the atomic theory that all matter is made up of atoms and molecules.

In 1924, an Indian physicist Satyendra Nath Bose sent Einstein a statistical model, which showed that light could be understood as a gas. When Einstein received this paper, he realised that this model, in addition to being applicable to photons, could also be used to describe atoms. Einstein added his views to the model, and together, they came up with the Bose-Einstein condensate phenomenon that appears at very low temperatures. This phenomenon gives rise to new particles called bosons. In 1995, the first such condensate was produced experimentally by Eric Cornell and Carl Wieman using ultra-cooling equipment at the University of Colorado at Boulder.

In 1926, Albert Einstein and former student Leó Szilárd co-invented the 'Einstein Refrigerator'. Though this was not one of his main interests, Einstein undertook this work as a way of helping a former student. He used the knowledge he had acquired during his years at the Swiss Patent Office to get valid patents for the invention in several countries. Though the refrigerator was not immediately put into commercial production, rights to use the patents were sold to companies such as Electrolux of Sweden. The funds obtained supported Szilárd for several years.

After his research on general relativity, Einstein focused on attempts to generalise his theory of gravitation to unify and simplify the fundamental laws of physics, particularly gravitation and electromagnetism. In 1950, he described this 'Unified Field Theory' in a *Scientific American* article titled 'On the Generalised Theory of Gravitation'.

In 1993, a Nobel Prize was awarded to the discoverers of gravitation waves. These waves were first predicted by Einstein. In 1995 a Nobel Prize was awarded to the discoverers of Bose-Einstein condensates. Einstein envisioned the presence of black holes before others and he was proved right. Today, astronomers have discovered thousands of black holes. And most important, many leading physicists are trying to complete Einstein's ultimate dream of a unified theory or a 'theory of everything.'

Towards the end of Einstein's days, most scientists began to work on the problems of quantum mechanics and not on relativity. Quantum mechanics studies the properties of atoms, and smaller particles like photons and electrons. This was because of the huge strides made by quantum theory in unraveling the secrets of atoms and molecules. Niels Bohr was one of the most influential quantum physicists, who proposed solutions to many questions in quantum physics. Einstein was unhappy with the 'Copenhagen interpretation' of the quantum theory developed by Niels Bohr and Werner Heisenberg. This theory said that quantum phenomena are 'inherently probabilistic', completely ruled by chance.

How could a man like Einstein, who believed in an orderly Universe, accept this? 'I, at any rate, am convinced that He [God] does not throw dice,' said Einstein!

He stayed unhappy with the quantum theory's description of nature till his death.

Einstein felt that Bohr's views on small particles (quanta) went against his own Theory of Relativity. However, experiments conducted since have confirmed that Bohr, rather than Einstein, was correct. Today quantum theory is one of the advanced subjects in science and has led even to novels like Timeline by Michael Crichton. This work of science fiction suggests that quantum theory, taken forward, can help people travel in time!

Though many people make out that Einstein and Bohr were enemies, it was not the case! Bohr was Einstein's closest friend. Bohr also provided answers to most of the challenges presented by Einstein. He was an intellectual equal. Their interaction was actually a friendly and fruitful series of exchanges of ideas.

Einstein the Pacifist and Humanist

Peace cannot be kept by force. It can only be achieved by understanding.

Einstein was not just a man of science, he was a strong believer in peace, and hated war and violence. That is why he was known as a pacifist.

Einstein's work was interrupted by World War I. For most of the war, he remained at the University of Berlin completing his general theory of relativity, but he was a staunch and outspoken opponent of the war. He had an aversion towards compulsory military service. Fortunately for him, he was no longer a German citizen.

Amidst all the strife, Einstein's was a voice of peace and reason. He was one of only four intellectuals in Germany to sign a manifesto opposing Germany's entry into war. Einstein was deeply upset by the spirit of war-hungry Germany. Disgusted, he called nationalism 'the measles of mankind.'

After the war, Germany was thrown into chaos and economic turmoil. During this time, in November 1918, radical students seized control of the University of Berlin and held the rector of the college and several professors hostage. There was great panic in the university and many people feared that calling in the police to release the officials would result in tragic confrontation and loss of life. Einstein, because he was respected by both students and faculty, was asked to talk to the students. Together with Max Born, Einstein brokered a compromise that resolved it.

Not for a moment should we think that Einstein was a coward who ran away from the battlefield. He said, 'I am not only a pacifist but a militant pacifist. I am willing to fight for peace. Nothing will end war unless the people themselves refuse to go to war.' This clearly showed that Einstein treasured peace so much that he was ready to fight for it. Einstein felt very strongly against war and he believed that people must make a conscious decision not to participate in or support war. He also strongly supported democracy and felt that social equality and economic protection should be the main priority of any government.

In the period between the two World Wars, the rise of the Nazi party in Germany led to the persecution of many Jews. Einstein was a Jew. Einstein's positive action resulted in the formation of the International Rescue Committee (IRC) in 1933. Its aim was to assist the opponents of Adolf Hitler. It helped Jews in Germany to escape maltreatment by the Nazi government. Its scope later expanded.

The IRC remains active till date, helping people fleeing from racial, religious and ethnic persecution, as well as those uprooted by war and violence.

At the start of the Second World War, Einstein learnt that some physicists in Germany had begun to contemplate developing a powerful atomic bomb based on his mass-energy equivalence principle. Fearing a catastrophe, he wrote to the American President Franklin D Roosevelt informing him of such research efforts. It was only then that the American government instituted a programme to develop an atomic bomb. This was known as the Manhattan Project.

Einstein, whose equation was the foundation of all this, was never asked to participate. This was probably because the American government knew that Einstein was a staunch pacifist who would never support the development of such a deadly weapon!

When the American army dropped an atom bomb on the Japanese cities of Hiroshima and Nagazaki, Einstein was appalled and saddened beyond words. Almost immediately, he became part of an international effort to try to bring the atomic bomb under control, forming the Emergency Committee of Atomic Scientists. He is supposed to have said that if only he had known that his discoveries in physics would have led to the making of something so terribly destructive, he would rather have become a watchmaker.

After the Second World War, Einstein lobbied with other like-minded friends to stop nuclear testing and future bombs. He was actively involved in these causes till the day he drew his last breath.

Einstein fought and campaigned for peace as he believed in human values. He had great belief in human rights. He felt 'the state is made for man and not man for the state.' Einstein felt that a person should be called upon to make only such sacrifices to the state as would promote the free development of individual human beings. Referring to compulsory military service, he said, 'The state violates the commandment that the state should be our servant and not the people its slaves when it compels us to engage in war, more so as the object and effect of this slavish service was to kill people belonging to other countries and thereby interfering with their freedom and development.'

More evidence of his compassion not only for human beings but also for animals was reflected in his belief in vegetarianism. He said 'It is my view that the vegetarian manner of living by its purely physical effect on the human temperament would most beneficially influence the lot of mankind.' In this, he was showing his understanding of other faiths in the world which believed that diet influenced human tendencies.

Einstein and India

Einstein had great regard for Mahatma Gandhi, Rabindranath Tagore and Gautama Buddha.

On Mahatma Gandhi, he said:

Generations to come, it may well be, will scarce believe that such a one as this (Gandhiji) ever in flesh and blood walked upon this Earth.

Einstein said this on the occasion of Gandhi's 70th birthday in 1939. This was before India's Independence. 'A leader of his people, unsupported by any outward authority, a politician whose successes rests not upon craft nor the mastery of technical devices but simply on the convincing power of his personality. A victorious fighter who has always scorned the use of force, a man of wisdom and humility armed with resolve and inflexible consistency, who has devoted all his strength to the uplifting of his people and the betterment of their lot. A man who has confronted the brutality of Europe with the dignity of the simple human being, and thus at all times risen superior,' is how he described the Father of the Nation.

Einstein's words were indeed prophetic. Gandhi's methods were successful. So, in 1950, three years after India's Independence and the Mahatma's tragic assassination (1948), he said in a United Nations radio interview, 'Taken on the whole, I would believe that Gandhi's views were the most enlightened of all the political men in our time. We should strive to do things in his spirit . . . not to use violence in fighting for our cause, but by non-participation in what we believe is evil.'

He felt Gandhi was unique in political history. He had invented an entirely new and human technique for the 'liberation struggle of an oppressed people' and had undertaken it with the greatest energy and devotion. He further felt that Gandhiji's philosophy would have a lasting value far beyond his own times, ruled by 'brute force'. Remember, Einstein witnessed two World Wars!

On Gandhi he once again said, 'We are fortunate and should be grateful that fate has bestowed on us so luminous a contemporary, a beacon to the generations to come.'

Asia's first Nobel Laureate, Rabindranath Tagore (Literature-1913), was an Indian with whom Einstein had a direct relationship. On 14 July 1930, Tagore visited Einstein in his home in Kaputh, Germany. It was a long conversation, during which they discussed God, religion and morality. While we all know of Tagore as a playwright, poet, writer who took part in the freedom struggle, this conversation reveals that he knew a lot about science too!

Three extracts from the conversation, give us insights into the minds of these two greats.

Einstein: 'Do you believe in the Divine as isolated from the world?

Tagore: Not isolated. The infinite personality of Man comprehends the Universe. This proves that the truth of the Universe is human truth. I have taken a scientific fact to illustrate this. Matter is composed of protons and electrons with gaps between. But matter may seem to be solid. Similarly, humanity is composed of individuals, yet they have their interconnections of human relationship. The entire Universe is linked up with us in a similar manner, it is a human universe.

Einstein: There are two different conceptions about the nature of the Universe. (1) The world as a unity dependent on humanity. (2) The world as a reality independent of the human factor.

Tagore: When our Universe is in harmony with man, the eternal, we know it as truth, we feel it as beauty.

Einstein: This is a purely human conception of the Universe.

Tagore: There can be no other conception. This world is a human world-the scientific view of it is also that of the scientific man.

Einstein: Truth, then, or Beauty, is not independent of Man?

Tagore: No.

Einstein: I agree with regard to beauty but not truth. I cannot prove scientifically that truth must be conceived as a truth that is valid independent of humanity; but I believe it firmly. The Pythagorean theory in geometry states that something is true, independent of the existence of man.'

In simple words, the two great men did not agree on what we call Truth. While the scientific genius felt that Truth existed independent of human beings, the philosopher insisted that Truth was present only within the understanding or mind of Man.

Einstein once said:

Our time is distinguished by wonderful achievements in scientific understanding and technical application of those insights. Who would not be cheered by this? But let us not forget that human knowledge and skills alone cannot lead humanity to a happy and dignified life. Humanity (should place those who proclaim) high moral standards and values above the discoverers of objective truth. What humanity owes to personalities like Buddha, Moses and Jesus ranks for me higher than all the achievements of the enquiring and constructive mind.

Einstein had strong views on religion, God and cosmic matters. A Jew, he respected other religions, especially Buddhism. This religion was born from the views of the great Indian saint, Gautama Buddha, who lived in the sixth century BC. To his followers, Buddha is God. Indeed, in one branch of Hinduism too, he is considered an incarnation of Lord Vishnu.

Einstein felt strongly that the Jewish scriptures, Jesus, the Buddha and other religious figures were important guides for the ethical advancement of humanity.

About Buddhism, he said that it had 'the characteristics of what would be expected in a cosmic religion for the future: It transcends a personal God, avoids dogmas and theology; it covers both the natural and the spiritual, and it is based on a religious sense aspiring from the experience of all things, natural and spiritual, as a meaningful unity. If there is any religion that would cope with modern scientific needs, it would be Buddhism.'

In other words, he liked Buddhism for not having strict rules, for looking at all aspects in a united manner and for its features which could tackle the needs of modern science.

Einstein and Religion

A knowledge of the existence of something we cannot penetrate, of the manifestations of the profoundest reason and the most radiant beauty, which are only accessible to our reason in their most elementary forms—it is this knowledge and this emotion that constitute the truly religious attitude; in this sense, and in this alone, I am a deeply religious man

Einstein, according to his own words was a deeply religious person. He was born a Jew and cherished the cultural values of Zionism through his life, but he did not believe in God the way many of us do. He believed that, 'God revealed himself in the lawful harmony of the world' and not in a 'God who concerns Himself with the fate and the doings of mankind.' In other words, Einstein did not feel that there was a God who decided the fate of the world or passed judgment. He rather felt God was seen in the order of the Universe. Though he was a Jew, he did not believe in the Judeo-Christian God. He did not believe a God who was only involved with those who believed in him.

Einstein felt science and religion could co-exist in harmony. He expressed the opinion that science was one of the best ways to reveal the structure of the Universe and thereby appreciate the wonders of God.

Einstein published an article in 1940 called *Science and Religion* which gave his views on the subject. In this he expressed the view that being religiously enlightened meant, 'that a person has liberated himself from selfish desires and is more involved with thoughts and feelings beyond him.' He did not feel that the acceptance of any Divine Being was necessary to be religious. Einstein also felt that the conflicts between science and religion had sprung from errors and misconceptions. He felt that while science and religion could not overlap, they depended on each other for many things. Einstein said, 'science without religion is lame, religion without science is blind ... a legitimate conflict between science and religion cannot exist.'

Einstein looked to bring together science and religion in his thoughts. He was deeply influenced by the teachings of Buddha and Spinoza. Spinoza was a Dutch philosopher of Portuguese Jewish origin. He was a rationalist. He did not believe in blind faith without knowledge. Spinoza said that God and Nature were two names for the same reality, a single substance. Einstein believed in this definition of God.

Einstein once compared education to a marble statue in a desert. If not continuously maintained and updated, it becomes weathered and featureless.

Memorable Einstein Quotes

Einstein had a fantastic sense of humour. Here are some well-known Einstein quotes.

'Any intelligent fool can make things bigger, more complex, and more violent. It takes a touch of genius—and a lot of courage—to move in the opposite direction.'

'Gravitation is not responsible for people falling in love.'

'The only thing that interferes with my learning is my education.'

'You see, wire telegraph is a kind of a very, very long cat. You pull his tail in New York and his head is meowing in Los Angeles. Do you understand this? And radio operates exactly the same way: you send signals here, they receive them there. The only difference is that there is no cat.'

'Sit with a pretty girl for an hour, and it seems like a minute. That's relativity.'

Einstein Timeline

1879	Einstein is born on 14 March
1881	Birth of his sister Maria
1884	Einstein and his family move to Munich
1885	Entry into school
1890	Exposure to religious education, phase of intense devotion to God
1894	Family moves from Munich to Italy leaving Einstein behind
1896	Einstein renounces German citizenship
and	becomes a Swiss citizen
1900	Einstein qualifies to study in Federal Institute of Technology, Zurich
1903	Einstein marries classmate Mileva Maric
1905	Einstein publishes 4 groundbreaking
papers	in science
1909	Einstein begins to do full time work in science

1914 Einstein separates from wife Mileva and family

1919 Einstein marries cousin Elsa Lowenthal

1920 Einstein recovers from his liver ailment

1921 Einstein visits United States to raise funds to set up a Hebrew University in Jerusalem
Einstein wins Nobel Prize in Physics

1928 Einstein gets Max Planck medal for contribution to quantum physics

1932 Einstein is appointed Professor in Institute of Advanced Studies, Princeton, USA

1933 Nazis come to power in Germany. Einstein is against them

1933-55 Spends rest of his life in Princeton and turns down request to become President of Israel

1940 Einstein publishes an article *Science and Religion*

1955 Einstein passes away due to a heart ailment

www.ingramcontent.com/pod-product-compliance
Ingram Content Group UK Ltd.
Pitfield, Milton Keynes, MK11 3LW, UK
UKHW040003200726
13854UKWH00001B/15